A Poet's Heart

A Poet's Heart

A collection of poems from the heart of a poet

Shanna L. Andersen

Thanks be to God, my Father in Heaven, for this gift I have been given, for all good gifts come from Him.

Dedicated to my wonderful husband, Thomas, without whom this book would not be. Thank you for encouraging and believing in me! Forever and Always, my love.

CONTENTS

Forward

My wife Shanna has always been inspired with her poems. Never has she been able to sit down and work through a poem but they always come to her in the moment just as they are supposed to be. They are what I would call inspiration, or a poem from heaven.

Poems unlike most any other kind of writing have simple rules that are meant to be changed all the time. My understanding about poems has gown drastically over the course of our marriage, and I've even written a few of them myself via the form of inspiration. One of which is dedicated to my wife Shanna and is included in this book, and was the inspiration for the title of this book.

If I could share anything to those who are going to read her poems is that she is sincerely genuine in her writing. The messages she has to offer are the raw preceding's of her heart. As you read I invite you to scan through the table of contents and choose to read them in the order you feel drawn to. Doing so gives you, as the reader a more full and enjoyable experience as Shanna shares her heart and inspiration with you.

And to my dear wife Shanna may you always write from your heart and share it with the world. I love you so much, and love your form of art.

A Poet's Heart

Time passes by
And soon we pass on
To a place no one can go
Full of stories untold

A Picture is worth a thousand words
And a book is filled with thousands
But each word that's in succession
Is a million thoughts of unique creation

For sometimes a simple phrase
Can change a world of hurt
And a poet's heart can seem untamed
When no one hears their art.

But to you my sweetie I hear your heart
And always and forever admire your art

- Thomas Andersen

The Story behind "A Hunger Unmet"...

One of my greatest desires for my life is to be able to see my lord and Savior face to face. This desire was so overwhelming one day that I just had to grab a pen and paper and let the words flow freely from my heart. This is what came out.

A Hunger Unmet

I have a great desire.
To stand before my God-face to face.
In the solitude of a mountain, I climb and reach the
pinnacle supreme.

A place to be apart from the world, their cares and
their ways.
They are not my people, for I am in truth a stranger
here.

I have wandered from exalted spheres and realms of
glorious light.
If all but my heart could clearly see what it is I
desire.

What do I hunger for the most?
The answer my spirit cries is to see my God, the Lord
of Hosts.

To be in His presence is so sublime, one cannot even
have words to find, to thread together from
beginning to end, not one coherent sentence formed
by moral tongue; yet, deep inside my spirit cries.
"My God, how great thou art!
How noble. How kind!" In the solace of a mountain
peak how I long to climb, that I myself might truly
find the longing of my heart.
To be with Thee, dear Lord of Lords and see the
King of Kings.
To reverence with my tears and praise with heart
and voice.

The Story behind "A Plea for My Soul"...

Just like everybody else I have weaknesses, we are meant to. One of my favorite scriptures is found in the Book of Mormon: Ether 12:27

"And if men come unto me I will show unto them their weakness, I give unto men weakness that they may be humble; and my grace is sufficient for all men that humble themselves before me; for if they humble themselves before me, and have faith in me, then will I make weak things become strong unto them."

This is Jesus Christ speaking. I have personally experienced this in my life. Our weaknesses can help us learn and grow. They can bring us closer to God if we apply His grace. I am often face to face with my weaknesses, as we all are, and one such time I just wanted to be free from all of it, I wanted to be Home. I wanted to be free from this Earth life. So, I wrote out this plea.

A Plea for My Soul

Oh how my soul grows so so weary of this mortal veil
of flesh.
Like my Brother Nephi, my heart is found
exclaiming, 'Oh, wretched man am I' How I grow
tired of the enemy of my soul.

My very flesh makes me an enemy to thee.
How I long to be full of light and love, to behold thy
holy courts above.

Father, Mother help cleanse me of all the sin that so
easily besets me.
Give me the grace of my Savior dear as I trudge
through these trenches of despair.

My fellow man I long to save with tenderness of
Mother, the love and strength of Father.
Instead I find the faults within their hearts that are
merely mirrors of my own.

Cast away these demons that fill me with dread.
Cast out, out, and away these devils that desire my
demise.
For though they know it not, they have only once
lived never to again.

Bear me upon the wings of angels kind and dear and
oh so near.
Fill my heart with longing to be again within thy
sight, to rule my actions both day and night.
Fill me with thy grace divine, and as thy light let me
shine.

The Story behind "Believe"...

As I receive personal revelation and inspiration I am often told to be believing. It is the number one thing that I am told. I often have a habit of doubting my answers to prayers and that I am hearing correctly. The whole time though, my Savior is just encouraging me to believe in myself. He tells me to believe that I am doing it correctly.

Believe

When my back is to a wall
No escape there seems to be
The only path to safety I see
Is to simply believe.

Though simple the solution be
Harder it is to instill
For this heart of mine longs to believe
But in unbelief is stony still.

To thee, my Lord and Savior
I lift up my weary voice
And with all the strength I can,
To the utmost muster
I cry out for but
One ounce of sweet relief.

Relieve me of this burden
How heavy a stony heart can be
Free me of these self-inflicted chains
Release me, oh please!

To no one else my heart will turn
Led by thee and thee alone

When now tempted I seem to be
To stare in blind unbelief
I choose to listen to His call,
"Believe, oh just believe."

The Story behind "Breaking Out of Prison"...

I recognize that I have been given this gift to write and share my heart through words. It was not until recently that I fully understood to what degree this gift has been given me. One day I was just so full of joy and words kept flowing that I was just in awe. It was then that I could see clearly that this is my gift and that I need to share it with the world. I was told that I have been given sacred words, but they do no good if they are stuck inside of me and not shared.

Breaking Out of Prison

How do I share this gift of which I have been given?
Of words that flow like milk and honey and swirl
deep within.

How do I break it free of the long stay in this prison,
built of pain and fear and my stubborn unbelief, not
of Him, but me?

How do I share so freely to bring them safely home,
to bring in Israel, scattered across the globe?

Into His open arms they come, carried upon the
words I write, of which He truly gives me.

Now, how? How do I set this free?
The answer that He clearly gives me now and
whispers into my heart and ear, "Do not look down in
doubt and fear. Simply trust in me."

The Story behind "Fireworks of the Soul"...

Often the process of receiving personal revelation (meaning answers to prayers, daily guidance for life, good feelings, etc.) is likened to receiving light. As I share in this poem I often find myself in the early morning seeking answers and guidance that I need. It is in these quiet hours that, as it is still dark outside and inside-as far as lack of knowledge- the revelation comes as a spark of light and often when once spark is received more will follow.

Fireworks of the Soul

Upon my knees in the still of morning. No bird song
to break the night, the stillness stretches on.

All the world is silent, quite- frozen it would seem
To allow the purest communication
From up above in the firmament of Heaven
To me, on this planet Earth below.

It is in these early hours, I seek
My Lord and Savior in sacred prayer
I seek to know divine truth
My highest truth, a jewel to me.

So in faith I ask, then I listen
To hear His long sought explanation.

The Spirit washes over me
From my head to my toes
And everywhere in-between.
Pure revelation received, illuminates the darkness

A spark
Then two, followed by
A third, A fourth, the light received
A firework to my soul

A burst of color, a revealing light
Followed by the boom
Reverberating my soul
Within my heart, my mind
Proof that it was there.

The Story behind "Fixing Broken Things"...

There was a period of time in my life where I thought I would marry a different guy. It didn't happen though, and at first I was devastated. Looking back now I am very grateful. He was a great guy, but Thomas is my one and only and always has been. That other guy is now married himself and happy, so it all works out. I wrote this right after we had had a conversation and I knew for sure that I would not marry him. My heart was completely broken.

Fixing Broken Things

I am good at fixing broken things
At least that is what some say.
A bit of glue
On broken shattered pottery
Good as new
What do you say?

A twist of my wrist
Driving a screw into a door
There, now
It shuts and opens
As it did before.

When it comes to my own heart
Can somebody help me?
No amount of
Glue
Tape
Or screws
Can help this beating broken heart.

It is the one puzzle
I cannot figure out.
Maybe you have a clue?

The Story behind "Forgiven"...

This poem was written at the moment my life turned around and my heart turned back to God.

I hadn't been going to church since the age of ten. There was an event that had occurred when I was eight years old that catapulted my life into the dark. I was doubting, lost, confused. By the time I was in High School I was doubting that God even existed.

I was lovingly lead back and started going to church again. I knew that I needed to repent and turn my life around, and that some of the things I had done in the past were not good. I had some things to fix and a deep desire to be clean and forgiven by God and myself.

The day I wrote this I had broken down in tears, just sobbing my heart out. I was full of Godly sorrow, not worldly sorrow. I was sad for what I had done and how I was because I knew they were contrary to the commandments of my God.

So I knelt down in prayer and through the tears I pleaded with God to forgive me. Immediately this overwhelming peace just enveloped me from head to toe and washed over me and through me all at once. I knew that my plea was heard, that I was forgiven, and I sat down and penned these words.

Forgiven

I am forgiven!
Oh, how sweetly my soul sings
In triumphant jubilation,
When my lips utter this sentence
With neither doubt in my heart
Nor bitterness upon my tongue.

The Story behind "He Was Always There"...

As I was away from the Restored Church and the simple, guiding truths of the Gospel of Jesus Christ I was full of confusion and fears. Now, being back in the fold of God I can see that my Savior was always there even if I couldn't see Him.

He Was Always There

It was Him
He stood right beside me
As I was encircled about
In impending despair.

For the dark storms
Those storms of confusion
Oh, how they racked
Havoc on my heart.

At times it was as if
I could feel my spirit
Being totally torn apart.

Letting out a shrill
Cry of anguish
It seemed to cry,
"This is not who we are
We are betraying our heart."

The cry was swallowed
In the storm's
Seemingly victorious roar.
Confusion ensued
Leaving me heavy with cares.

It was His voice I heard
Speaking softly and clear,
"You know there is more to life.
Lift up your head, hold on your way
Oh, do not fear."

At the sound of His voice
My spirit revived
And let out a hopeful cry.

It was His hand
Leading me back into the safety of the fold
And as I sat within those walls
It was His love
That told me I was finally home.

My spirit sung a sweet lilting song
A tune of hope
Of love
Of freedom found and freedom won.

Now, within the light
I look back on my plight.
I see the beauty there
Of my Savior's tender care.

For though I was blind to see
His sweet beautiful grace
He was always with me keeping
This one lost sheep
Secure and safe.

Never once out of His sight
Was I?
No, for He was always there
Forever by my side.

The Story behind "Hero"…

Growing up I was super close to my dad. He was amazing to me and still is. I am a big Daddy's girl. I wrote this poem for him on a Father's Day card that I made for him when I was in High School. He still to this day remembers it.

Hero

Whether I am frightened or sad
I run to him.
May it be a monster under the bed,
Or tears to shed
I go to him.

He takes me in welcoming arms
Where my worries
Flutter and fly
Free in the breeze.
He listens without question
Never does he fail
To cheer me up when tears
Are unwanted.

He may not be Superman
Or the incredible man.
He may not climb a tree to save that cat
Or save a person from
A wrathful fire.

He may not be able to fly,
To fight off ten thousand men,
But he is a hero to me.

He is
The most incredible person
With so much heart
With so much soul.

If I have a crumby day
Or if I just don't know
What to do or say,
He is always there.
He picks me up,
Catches my tears,
He chases away all my fears.

He is my buddy
My shield
He is my life
And he is my favorite Superhero.
He is my dad.

The Story behind "I am a House Plant"...

I had just returned home from a full time mission for the Church of Jesus Christ of Latter-day Saints in Las Vegas, Nevada. I was living in Boise, Idaho with a family that I was working for as a live-in nanny. Elisabeth, the Mom, became a friend to me. She, being a poet herself, was always encouraging me to write.

One day I was in the hot tub room where there were some potted plants. I noticed that one of them was so big, but still inside the small little original pot it had come in. It was so big it was almost tipping over from the weight of the plant itself. So, I decided to transplant it. I grabbed a bigger pot and put soil in it and placed the plant inside its new home. It seemed happier there, even though it was new and a lot bigger.

Something whispered to me that I am like that plant. I used to be in a very familiar world-small and comfy, but now I am in a new place, a new job, a different car, new people, and everything is bigger and a little bit scarier, but I was finding that I now had room to grow into the person I am today.

I am a House Plant

I repotted a house plant today
And removed it, roots and all
I wanted to give it a way
To grow up and out and tall.

In God's garden
I am that house plant
I sit comfy in the same little spot
To Him no bigger than an ant
But tenderly He lifts me up,
He plants me in a much bigger spot.

Up, He pulled me
Up with my roots.
Now I have so much more room
I have room to grow
To become all that He knows
I can truly be.

And you know something?
It is not as scary
Not so scary as I thought
I find I actually like it here
In my big new pot.

The Story behind "I Am Me"...

As I was on my mission a bunch of us Missionaries would meet together on our P-day (stands for preparation day. The one day out of the week that we have to do our laundry, write our families, clean our apartments, and do anything else we need to.) And play basketball or some other sport, just for fun.

On one of these days everybody else was playing ball and having fun, but I just wasn't feeling it. I instead sat off to the side and wrote letters to my family and friends. While I was writing I felt a little awkward and I had this moment of wondering why I am like this. Why am I so different from everybody else? The words, "I needed you, so be you" came into my mind and then the words of this poem.

We can only compare ourselves with ourselves and nobody else. We are us for a reason and the World needs us, not us trying to be like everybody else.

I Am Me

I am me.
For a divine reason this is so.
I am here to reach people
In Fall, Summer, Winter, and Spring.

At my core
Music and Love
Virtuous and pure
Nothing stays that I do not want there.

I choose not to
Partake of all the worldly things
Rather I stand.
I stand as me-
Stalwart, valiant, free.

To be known of man
This was never my desire.
I stand with my Savior and
What I am to Him
Is what I want to be.

I might seem peculiar
But truly I am me
And I stand tall in this peculiarity.

I am a daughter in His kingdom
More precious than
Diamonds and rubies.
I know who I am
And I let her be
Day by day by day.

The Story behind "I Find You there"...

We went to a faith-based expo. There were all sorts of different presentations and classes going on. At the start of one of them I asked the presenter a question. I thought that would be the end of it, but then after the class the Presenter's assistant came and sat next to me and proceeded to answer my question and take the time to explain some things to me. I could feel such love as she did this. I could feel my Savior's love for me and it just filled my soul. I took a moment to give thanks for the experience and then recorded it as well, and as I was doing so these words came flowing out.

I Find You There

I hear your voice through others
Between their lips they speak
The words that, if you were here,
I know you'd speak to me.

They lift and carry a spirit so weary
Of feeling so lost and apart
Left to journey this life, so lone and dreary
And in your presence I am not.

What hope it brings into my soul
Into my very heart
To know that in a world so cold, so dark
Your light is there within the tiniest of sparks.

Your guiding hand. Your warm embrace
Is found right there within
The stranger's inspired hug
In the whispered words of love.

How kind thou art
How loving and sweet!
My soul is bound to proclaim
My God, how great thou truly art.

Through all my days you provided a way
To stay and walk with me.
Truly you are there in the company of others.
I find you in a kind smile
I find you in the words that strangers kindly speak.

The Story behind "I Have Your Back"...

On my mission we were teaching this man about the Atonement of Jesus Christ (When He suffered in the Garden of Gethsemane, died on the cross, and was resurrected) I had the inspiration to liken it to a war. The man we were teaching, Wes, had been in the Marines, so he would be able to relate. It was one of the most powerful, heart-touching times on my mission. The Spirit of God bore witness to all of us that what I was explaining was true. We all felt the beauty of the Atonement and the love of a Father in Heaven who would give His only Begotten Son for all of us, so that we can be cleansed from sin, enabled to return to live with Him again.

I Have Your Back

I trudge through this land.
Marching one, two. One two.
Another Soldier in this war.
A number and nothing more.

Listening to orders and fulfilling commands, with
nothing on my tongue except a quick, "yes sir!"
My brothers beside me have been shot and disarmed.
This life is so fragile, one moment here and the next
gone.

I keep marching through sand and through heat.
The only reality being my gun in my hand and the
beat of the bright burning sun.

A bullet is fired, followed by a second and third.
Quick, take cover!
Screams a warning unheard, before you join your
brothers deep down in the dirt.

A fourth bullet fired.
Too late to duck and cover.
I am down. I am hit.
Oh man, is this it?

Will I live to see my wife, to be by her side?
Will I get to hold my daughter and listen to her
laugh or listen to her cry?
Down in the dirt I lie, I guess it is my turn to die.

But what is this?

I am being lifted up from the rubble and up from the
dirt. Someone holds me close and carries me through
the raging war.
Through my baggage and all that was before.

Who is this person?
I do not understand. Is it my buddy, my brother,
come back to with me stand?

He lays me down in a safe place to hide.
He takes off my vest, helmet, and pack.
He picks up my gun and puts it away, freeing my
hand from fighting today.

A careful hand, gentle and kind, tends to the wound
that is now in my side.
A prick of pain I feel here and there, but I do not
worry for I know it will heal with his tender care.

With the weight of my vest relieved from my chest, I
feel lighter than air, no longer oppressed.
I lay down my head, and as I do so, my rescuer
speaks and tells me these truths:

Do not worry, I am here.
I will not disappear.
I will fight this battle for you so you will not dare.

Rest and know that you are safe in my care.
Safe in my arms, and safe in my love.
You do not have to do this useless fighting anymore.

Your life is so much grander than this gun in your hand. For you there is a purpose, for you there is a plan.

I am your Savior, your brother, your very best friend. I will be by your side through the thick and the thin.

When the bullets come flying I will shield you again. Know, my dear brother, I will never leave you uncovered ever again.

I have your back, now take my hand.

The Story behind "In these Shoes"...

      Missions are hard. They are meant to stretch you and try you to help you grow and mature spiritually. A full-time missionary for the Church of Jesus Christ of Latter-day Saints spends 18-24 months in a foreign land. You are assigned another missionary to be with you at almost all times and you don't always get along with that person- this person is called a companion. Missionaries teach people the restored gospel and help others come unto Christ. They are away from home and their families for that whole time, some for the first time. They devote that whole time to the Lord for the building up of the Kingdom of God upon the Earth.

      One of my companions was having a hard time on her mission and wanted to go home. We ran into our mission Mom (the Mission President's wife), Sister Neider one day. She likened a mission to a new pair of shoes. When you first get them you want to take them off because they hurt your feet, but soon those shoes get broken in and they become your favorite pair of shoes. This is surely what happens on a mission for most Missionaries.

In these Shoes

New shoes pinch and poke
Causing blisters to form and feet to hurt
In this foreign environment
My feet long to be free.

Slowly, bit by bit
Inch by inch
My feet become acclimated
Quite comfortable
No longer pinched.

A few many miles to go
I find myself asking
"How am I to walk on this long path ahead?"
Take one step, and one step more.

With each step I take
My shoes become beaten
Broken
More comfy
More home.

Only a few steps left to be journeyed
On this path stretched
Right out before me
My journey coming to a close.

Once new shoes
No longer are new
Faded from the sun
Warped form the heat

They are comfy
They are now a very part of me.

These, my shoes
Have helped me see
What life really is.
I stand taller
And wiser
And overall better
From the journey
That I have traveled in these shoes.

Must I take off these shoes?
A very part of me now?
Cannot I wear them?
If only for a little bit longer?

I have grown in these shoes
I have climbed mountains
In these, my shoes
I have even discovered
Who I am in these shoes.

A journey of self-discovery
An exploration of my identity
In these shoes
I have walked
Where I have never walked before.

The Story behind "Lost & Found"...

I had been searching for a specific answer and one day I had a vision. In my mind's eye I saw a room with the curtains drawn back, allowing the beautiful rays of sunlight to shine in. The rays of light seemed to be pointing to a table in the middle of the room. On the table sat a beautiful jewel that was brilliantly shinning. I then knew that that represented my answer, and then I knew what the answer was. I had found it.

Lost & Found

Lost within the voices
That swirl around in my head
I only desire to follow where
By Thine hand I am lead.

Conflict. Confusion.
Swirling grey and black
As I try, try, and try
To hear the truth I lack.

Lost Within the beat
Of my own heart
And of my mind being swayed
I know though, who I listeth to obey.

I follow my Savior
The Lord Jesus Christ.
With an ounce of faith
I seek out the light.

The windows are open
The curtains drawn back.
Within the rays of light
Lays the answer to find.

Just one simple sentence
It was there all along
Lost it was.
Swept away by the swirling throng.

Found is the answer
To follow with all of my heart.
To speak those words
Without fear
Without doubt.

I follow my Master
The Bright Prince of Peace.
He it is who leads me
Direction and guidance by His hand
I gladly receive.

Found I am.
The purpose is in mind.
I know what I must do now
The lost has been found.

The Story behind "Make Me Pure"...

There is a song that we sing in Church titled, "More Holiness Give Me" the third verse says,

"More purity give me/ more strength to o'er come More freedom from earth stains/ more longing for home.
More fit for the kingdom/ More used would I be More blessed and holy/ More Savior like thee."
-   Philip Paul Bliss

I long to be free from the earth stains that smudge my soul. This was my plea.

Make Me Pure

Oh, purify me, my Lord.
Wring from
My heart
My body
My mind
Wring from my soul
And all of me
The darkness that holds me
From being me.

Burn out the dross
Along with the refuse
Make me clean
Make me new.

This is the hope
I grasp and cling onto
Oh make me pure
Even as thou art
That one day I may stand
At thy feet
To see thee face to face.

The Story behind "Missing a Friend"...

I wrote this poem at the same time as "Fixing Broken Things" so this too is about that guy I thought I would marry. When we said our goodbyes I was mostly sad because I knew that when I did get married he and I wouldn't be friends anymore. It would just be awkward. That was the saddest part. I was missing him a lot one day and I wrote this poem.

Missing a Friend

Missing a friend is like...
Being a ship without a trusty Captain.
Gone ashore, nobody on board.
Left to drift no more, no purpose anymore.

Missing a friend is like...
Being a bird
Flightless, captive, And frightened
Unable to soar
Into the infinite blue expanse of sky.

Like not being able
To smell the rain
In the midst
Of the thunder.

Like not seeing
The silver lining
In every cloud
That passes right on by above.

Or...
Not feeling
The earth between your tooo
Below.

Missing a friend
Is like...
A puzzle without
That one missing piece
Never ever complete.

The Story behind "More Than Self"...

I do not care what others might think. I know
that the Founding Fathers were good and inspired
men. America is a free country because of them and
the men who fought bravely for them and every other
military leader through U.S. history. They really did
think more of the possibility of and the, then new
nation, than they did of themselves. On the fourth of
July I wrote this to honor them.

More than Self

The price of freedom is a steep one.
With blood freely spilt freedom was won.
The blood of those good men, whom more than self,
their country loved.
Little is known on a personal level, the sacrifices
made amidst the struggle.

The Founding Fathers, the leaders of volunteer
armies. To them we give our thanks, on this our day
of independence.
No thought of self was ever theirs.
To the cause of liberty they took up arms; at times
with pen and others powder.

Theirs was a cause all too noble.
The tears cried by their children and wives sanctified
the sacrifice.
Unknown was the fate of their Fathers, husbands,
and friends.
Unknown was the outcome of such valiant and noble
efforts.

Why? Some blatantly ask. Why all of the strife?
Was it worth it?
Why give their lives?

A legacy they left of courage, strength, and absolute
trust in the Living God,
For it is in God we trust.
"For Liberty!" was their cry.

A declaration that pushed them forward, through
thick and thin.
Over hill and dale.
Through the known and uncertain.
More than self, they fought for liberty.

In another place, a different time,
Far before these great men,
This plea was heard, not again but first.
In the garden that night, on bended knees,
Was our Savior, Redeemer.
Giving His life for us.
Suffering in the utmost extremes.

Why? Some would exasperatedly cry.
Was it worth it?
Why would He give His life?
"For Liberty." was His cry.

Freedom from death and sin.
He set us free from Justice's demand;
Freedom to Reconciliation.

All for us, more than self.

The Story behind "Mother in Heaven"...

It was Mother's Day and I was sitting in Church. I had the thought: 'how many people think about Heavenly Mother on Mother's Day?'

If God is our Heavenly Father, the Father of our Spirits, then we must have a Heavenly Mother as well, for this Earth life and the relations here are a mirror of those in the Heavens. I know that Father loves me, so then I know that Mother does too. I wrote this to Her.

Mother in Heaven

Mother in Heaven, It is on this day
I choose to express my greatest gratitude.
It was there by your side
Before this earthly life
I learned to love and grow by faith.

Your nurturing ways taught me
To always be gentle
To be kind
And ever more like thee.
From you I learned
What it is to be woman.
From you I learned
My role of divinity.

On this day
I thank you
Even though you are no longer with me,
Your presence is absent,
Your influence is vital to my life
As I am upon this Earth.

Your sacred identity is void
No longer in my memory
And shroud from my eyes.
Each time I look
Within myself
I see who you must be
A woman of
Truth
Light
A woman of love
A sacred Deity.

How much Father loves you
To keep you
From all this earthly profanity.
I look forward to the day
Where I get to see you once more
Then I shall remember my Mother in Thee.

The Story behind "Music"...

I wrote this poem in High School. I have always enjoyed good music, and this was just a fun little poem that I wrote.

Music

Music is all around us
In this world that we see
Delighting our ears
Caressing our minds.

A solo trumpet on
A luminescent city street
A guitar everybody goes to meet.

The sounds of city streets and more
A moonlit wave crashing on the distant shore.

Ballads romance us
The blues speak to us.

No matter where you are
Music is flowing.
In a little French restaurant
Where the candles are glowing.

A Japanese garden
With Lotus flowers and dragons
No matter where you are
Music will find you.

Music is the World's language
Irish jigs and African drums
You need not speak the language
To understand.
Music opens your mind
You soul and heart.

Every song has a feeling
Sorrow or joy
Every song tells a story
Of love or surrender.

Anytime and anyplace
Relax and listen
Release your worries
Open mind and ears
And listen
To the stories.

The Story behind "My Chains Fall Free"...

When I was pregnant with our second son I struggled with post-partum depression all over again. It was hard and I felt like I was on a roller coaster of emotions often. One of those days was my hardest yet and I was not myself at all. So many nasty and dark thoughts were swirling inside of me that I couldn't get rid of. A black cloud seemed to settle right on top of me and I felt like I couldn't do anything about.

I remember laying on my bed, not being able to move even a finger, just feeling crushed. I knew deep down that I had to do something. The only thing that I could do- that I had the strength to do was silently call out to my Father in prayer.

As soon as I did a vision was opened up to me. I saw myself in a deep dark pit. I was bound with heavy thick ropes. I had a gag in my mouth and was being held down by demons, who were holding the ends of the ropes.

As soon as I called out for help I saw an angel. He was wearing white flowing clothing and held a sharp, flaming sword. His luster was brilliantly white and blinding as it shone into the pit. He quickly sliced through the ropes and took the gag from my mouth. My captors hissed in disgust and fled away from the angel of light. The vison closed and I was myself once more.

My Chains Fall Free

Bound. Trapped.
Entangled within feet and feet
Of chains of obsidian.
Tight ropes leave no slack
As I struggle they constrict.

The mocking jeers
The snide laughter
Emanates from amidst my captors.

Pinned to my bed
In the throes of despair
Neither the hope of light
Nor of goodness is there.

Is there no rescue to be found?
Here I lie gagged and bound
Is there a friendly hand
To save me from myself?

I struggle and pull
Trying to escape, but only in vain
From their nets and pain
All of the pain

Darkness closed in
Confusion was winning.
It was then that I remembered
To call on my Father.

He had been waiting

Just waiting patiently
For my move of faith
To call upon His name.

In a moment of freedom of voice
I called out to my Father
I called out by choice.
I only could muster
The courage to utter
Three simple words.
"Help me Father!"

As the words left my lips
To my eyes a vision was opened
An angel-majestic and glorious
He came to my aid
Brandishing a sword of pure light
As bright as the sun
Brilliant and bright

He slashed and he broke
All the chain and the rope.
Freeing me enough to banish the rest.

The darkness was lifted
The light fluttered in
Into my mind
Into my heart
That though bruised
Still beat within my chest.

Redemption came with drops
Precious drops of His blood.
With a drop of my faith

He freed me and
My chains fall free.

The Story behind "Nature's Melodious Music"...

   I have been taking Voice lessons from a friend. She has me do all sorts of different things after each lesson for homework. One of those assignments was to write a poem about the music of the seasons and within nature. This was for her.

Nature's Melodious Music

With the change of season
Brings the spirit
And melodious sounds
Of Nature's music.

The serenade of
Crickets and frogs
Will soon fade
In its place
A symphony of a different array.

As the warm temperature changes
For cooler, crisper degrees
The leaves will change from
Green making way to
A splendid display
Not one color—
But many now blow in the wind
Orange and brown
Purple and crimson
Some are even golden.

The crinkle and crunch
With every whisper of wind
Or under the feet
Of the bundled up human.
These are the notes
Sent away on the breeze
And are now being whistled
By the wind through the trees.

Even colder yet
The year will become
With it brings carols
Of sleighs and of bells
And the crunch
Of tightly packed snow.

If you are quite
And ever so still
You shall hear
The hushed little whisper of
The fresh snow fallen
Straight from the heavens.

It falls oh so softly
And flittering flies
And lies in the light
Of the bright glowing lamp.

Now Christmas is here
To celebrate
The world of nature
Stand still.
"Peace, peace"
She whispers to us
"Our Savior is here."

A soul-stirring
Acapella number is sung
By a single star
High in the Heavens.
So sacred, so pure
Only the angels shall hear.

The Story behind "My Testimony"...

When I first came back to the Restored
Church and new in the gospel again I felt like my
testimony was so tiny compared to everyone else's. I
was surrounded by Grandparents and friends who
knew more and felt more than I did. I wanted to be
like them in my faith.

My Testimony

Right now as I write these words
My testimony is like that
Of a young tree sprout.
It peeks above the ground
Just barely
To peer up at the giants surrounding it,
Hoping to someday
If possible mirror them all.

The tiny sprout reaches to the sky
It is seeking nourishment from the light.
I feed it
And with my faith
I know
If I pray my sprout will grow
A little at a time.

A tree it will become
Even a tree with
A protective canopy
Under which my children will recline
To find a truthful peace.

The Story behind "Ode to Cody"...

My family lived in Alaska. We moved there when I turned two years old and left when I was turning six. My Dad's boss asked us if we could watch his dog- a yellow lab- for him while he was away. Being the animal lovers that we are and having a dog ourselves we gladly accepted. We watched him for a time and when his owner came back Cody peed on the floor, ran upstairs, and hid under one of our beds. My dad's boss saw how much Cody didn't want to go with him and loved us, so knowing that he didn't have the time that he needed for the dog, he said that we could keep him. Oh, how we loved that dog. Neil was the one who rescued him from the Pound when he was a pup.

Ode to Cody

Abandoned. Alone.
And time ticking on by.
A hand pulled you in the nick of time.
Saved, our miracle dog.

Tracks in the snow
Sledding, happy and free
He went away
You came to stay

A garbage disposal on four legs.
Bananas, carrots, and bread
Down the hatch they went.
Red-velvet soft ears upon your head
Chocolate-brown seal eyes.
A gentle, Peaceful,
Heart of gold.

Jumping the fences
Beach runs in the sun
A true buddy for some fun
Chasing wild horses.

White face with young ears
Conquering all of your fears
Slower walks down in the woods
You were so good.

Thank you Cody
For a joyful time
Now we have said goodbye
Our miracle dog,
Chase those wild horses.

The Story behind "Nature's Midnight Musical"...

My Grandparents-Oma and Opa we would call
them, had the most wonderful home in Bose. It was
right along the Green Belt, next to a canal, and
tucked back and away from the main street within
the neighborhood. It was a haven for all of the
animals around. They would feed the ducks cracked
corn, all the little birds seed, and even put corn cobs
on a little see saw that my Opa made for the
squirrels. I love animals and nature, so growing up it
was a magical place to be.

One of the bedrooms upstairs was called the wildlife
room and was appropriately decorated to match.
There were stuffed animals on bookshelves, pictures
on the walls, and even fun fishy sheets on the bed,
which was a pull out hiddabed. If you opened the
back window at night you could hear all of the
nighttime animals, which was such a delight to me.

Nature's Midnight Musical

Outside my window
The dancers take their places
The musicians tune their instruments
They are all anxiously waiting
Wanting to perform.

The curtain of Yesterday goes up
Midnight heralds in
The start of the show
Ladies and Gentlemen please be seated.

The wind leads the trees
Into a whirl of a dance
Leaving my ears all in a trance.

The dancers are bending
They are swaying in the breeze
Their leaves whisper
About many secret things.

A bubbling creek is humming
A tune
A constant throughout
This mystical production.

The percussionists are frogs
Belting out
One, two
One, two.
Their thrumming echoing
Ricocheting off the trees
Being sent away
Adrift on the breeze.

All the dancers
The drummers
The singers
Do their various parts
To help nature come together.

Under the canopy of stars
The ray of moonshine
They continue to play out the show
Until the dim glow of sunrise.

Outside my window
At the stroke of Midnight
There opens a show
Of Nature's surprise.

The Story behind "Opening the Door"...

The person I am so grateful for is my cousin, Heather Dransfield. She is the one who courageously brought me back into the fold of God. She was the one who asked a simple question, extended a simple invitation. She is the angel in this poem. This poem is a metaphorical journey with her, not a literal one.

Opening the Door

Once I stood outside a door
In the cold of night
Thinking to myself, there must be more
Isn't there more meaning to my life?

No moon was there up in the sky
To guide my search
For the key that was right.
But what did my eyes behold?

A saint, an angel
Watching me with one eye.
Said I to her,
"May I please borrow some light?"

She glided right over
To where I stood.
Then said she to me,
"The key is uncovered."
Puzzled, I glanced down and then understood.

Laying right there
On the Welcome mat
Where once was void
Now there sat
A key-
Matching the lock exact.

I picked it up
Walked to the door.
The angel stopped me and said,
"Necessary is the key no more."

She simply glided to the door
She pushed it open wide
And I went falling
As I stumbled inside
Into the light.

Inside the room
A fire sat burning
I saw a table laden with food
The sight of which set my soul-
Oh, how my soul was yearning.

The angel spoke to me once more,
"Behold, the key is useless
As you only had to believe
For the hidden light
To be unleashed."

The Story behind "Prayer"...

Prayer is a gift! I am so grateful to be able to talk to my Father in heaven on a daily, hourly basis. Prayer is simple. He wants us to come to Him as any Father wants to hear from his child. He wants to know our thoughts, our fears, our dreams, and he just wants us to share our hearts with Him. This is also how we ask for the things we need and the things we want.

The KJV of the Bible has the definition for payer as such:

"Prayer is the act by which the will of the Father and the will of the child are brought into correspondence with each other. The object of prayer is not to change the will of God but to secure for ourselves and others blessings that God is already willing to grant but that are made conditional on our asking for them."

"Ask, and ye shall receive; knock, and it shall be opened up unto you."

Prayer

Talking with my Heavenly Father
Any hour of the day
Asking for forgiveness
For the things
I think
And do
And say.

He knows I am not perfect
But still I approach in faith.

I fold my arms and bow my head
This is how I connect to Him
I know He is there
Silently listening to my plea
To my mind
My heart and soul.
Be thou worthy of His counsel?

Keep His commandments
Remember His Son
Ask in Jesus' name
And it shall be done.
Thou shalt receive what thou wouldst want
Even what thou wouldst need.

The Story behind "Scars"...

Due to complications both our boys were breech resulting in caesarean births. So I have some scars. One day after the birth of our second son, Talmage, I had the thought that my scars are a lot like the scars of our Savior in that they both were a result of bringing life into the World.

Scars

I have this scar within my navel
To life he came
And here it shows.
It is much like yours.

The price for bringing life
Into this fallen world.

Mine is not within my side
Sometimes still, I feel it there.

Where your hands held nails
Mine hold this precious life-
A baby
So pure, so fine.

He is free to live
Because of the price.
The price you gladly paid
So that we would be free
For love and for life.

The Story behind "Taking off the Mask"...

As I was in High School I was so shy and the
"loner" you could say. I had no self-confidence and
cared way too much about what others thought about
me, but what teenager doesn't? Coming back to
Church and to God helped me with that confidence
and helped me see my divine nature. I am important
and of worth despite what others think, so I am just
going to be myself. I am not going to wear the "mask"
any longer.

Taking Off the Mask

I used to wear a mask
Upon my face it lay
It wasn't made of plaster
It wasn't made of lace

I wore it to hide
All of my secret feelings inside
To protect my heart
From being crushed
To just stay alive.

With it life was easy
It fit so naturally
But then it started to
Smother me
Constraining me.
My protection turned into my pain.

One day with confidence found
I yanked it off
I cast it to the ground.
No longer in a cage
No longer afraid.

Now, these days I feel
The warm sun on my face
And now I know
What it means to be me
Fearless and free.

The Story behind "The Beauty of Life"...

I wrote this one when I was in high School as well. It was my Senior year when I was trying to figure out what I wanted to do with my life. So many paths to choose from. I love puzzles and mystery stories.

The Beauty of Life

The beauty of life is the unknown.

If we knew what was to be
Around every twist and bend
In the journey
We wouldn't strive to do our best
We wouldn't learn from
Our mistakes,
The past.

We would be bored
Hindsight would be dead.
Worry and Stress wouldn't be alive,
But neither would
Satisfaction
Improvement
Or Progression.

The mystery of figuring it out:
What to do
Where to go
Who to love
Is what life is all about
Living.

Mystery is the beauty of life.

The Story behind "The Essence of Me"...

I was writing to my mom on a P-day when I was on my mission and this is what came out. I told her "I think you just got my next poem." I hadn't even planned it. It just came out this way.

The Essence of Me

As I go about this work my heart is tender
With ever-flowing love
That courses through my veins
Almost as if it were a brightly burning flame
With all the colors you can name.

It lights up my soul and enlightens my mind
This love that I hold is ever expanding
Causing my heart to change
Causing it to grow.

Even in the dark that flame
Is always there
Even in the bleak of night
In the dreariest of days
That flame of my love is always the same.

It is intertwined with my spirit
The very essence of who I am.

This flame of vibrant array
That burns inside me day by day
Shedding its beams of warmth and light
As if it were the sun
The very sustenance to life.

This flame is me
It is who I am
This flame is my core
Without I would float
Like a teardrop in space
Up, up and...away.

The Story behind "The Photo"...

When I was in High School I liked photography. I enjoyed taking pictures and my sister, Rachel and I would often be catching different scenes or views. It was fun. This was just a fun little poem that I wrote.

The Photo

A fragment of life is captured
In a flash
From a click of a button
A moment- frozen- in time.

They say a picture is worth a thousand words
Then why when you look at them
The words do not come?
Left speechless is one.

Take a glimpse into people's lives
Feel the emotions in the faces, so alive
Fear and joy
Passion and depression
Feel alive
Feel free to be what you want to be.

From the moment the shutter opens
The world is your paint
The camera your canvas
You are the Artist.

The Story behind "The Something Inside"...

Everybody has a must. Your must is what you are here to do, what you must do while on this Earth. I wrote this poem as a gift for my Dad. I knew that I had to. I still, to this day, am not sure why but I did.

Interesting thing is as I was writing this poem I figured out what my must is. Surprise! It is writing. Somehow I hadn't quite figured this out until I wrote this poem. Funny how that happens.

The Something Inside

Once there was a quiet something inside that lead your steps, stride for stride.

The something inside didn't need to shout or shake. It didn't need to stomp as if in a parade. Something inside of your beating heart was heard, listened to and honored.

Until one day, somehow and some way, as you grew up and childhood fleeted away, you shut up that something. You locked it away.

Something Inside isn't just a fleeting thought or a mere acquaintance.
This something inside is your must, the very purpose to your life.

The drive and electricity flowing through your batteries, charging you from head to toe. It is the call you have been given, in a way it is your mission; the meaning to your days, must is the essence of your soul.

There are those voices within and the voices without that surround you with lies so cunningly whispered.

They pester and hound you and deafen your ears to the pleas of that little, not quit defeated voice.

Hear. Can you listen to that ever soft plea of the Something Inside? That voice that cries from deep down inside.

Ready, it is to take one more stand. To, with courage found and strength mustered, lift up its voice and sound its demand.

"I matter," it says, practically whispers," I matter and really need you to listen. If only you knew what you and I could do. If only you listened to me too."

As we honor the must inside of us we live out life. The life we simply didn't know could mean so much to us. The life we kept only inside, the dream that we steadily dreamed at night.

It has been said that a painter must paint; a writer must write. These are their musts that live within them, bold and bright.

Now, what is the must that dreams of coming into the light?

What is that something, the Something Inside?

The Story behind "The Truth Is"...

   I saw lack of self-worth and confidence in somebody close to me and it reminded me of myself as a teenager. I have since learned that nothing diminishes our worth or adds to it, we came with it and it is eternal. Satan tries to get us to hate ourselves and each other by envy, but we are always enough because our Savior is enough. We are us and we are worth more than rubies to our Father in Heaven. He loves each of us so much, yes, even you.

The Truth Is

It is a lie.
That your worth is in-
Your beauty
Your achievement
Your talent.

A lie that you
Are not worthy of-
Love
Forgiveness
A reason to smile.

The truth is this:
The worth of souls is great.
We are who we are
He loves us for that.

Souls do not have
Size
Shape
Or even age.

They are eternal
They are boundless
Not confined
To how we might define.

The truth is this-
The One who made you
Loves you regardless
Of the scuff marks on your soul

Of the scars on your heart.

Saved and redeemed
Liberated with a price.
A price paid in full

A precious currency
The demands were paid
Not with gold nor diamonds.
Not with pounds or some yen.

Paid with the drops
Of red, red crimson.
The blood that flowed free
In the Garden that night.

The Price was paid by Him
Who was willing to pay.
He loved us enough
He believed in us enough
He is enough.

He prayed for you
He prayed for me
And through the mounting agony
He prayed for the eternities.

So next time you are tempted
To say you are not enough
Whatever it is
Still the truth is
You are because He is.

The Story behind "Thy Will Be Done"...

The only way that I have found to have lasting joy is to keep the commandments of God, remember my Savior, Jesus Christ and live as He did. I don't want to do my will, but His for in doing that I know I will grow, progress, and become more than I thought I could. Not to mention have joy in this life.

"Men are, that they might have joy." – 2 Nephi 2:25 The Book of Mormon

Thy Will Be Done

I throw my hands up
High into the air
I no longer care
To listen.

So many voices contest
To lead me away and astray
Further and further
From the path back Thy way.

I am done relying upon
The weakness of flesh
In my own strength
I am lost
It would seem to be
To my own understanding

I will be brave
To step out into the darkness
Though it seems to go on a ways
I trust and I take Thee
As my guide

No longer just listening for my will
As Thy daughter
Instead I listen for Thee
As my Father.

So that I,
Like my Captain of old
May say within my soul
"Not my will
But Thine be done.

The Story behind "To Ireland"...

I had the opportunity to visit Ireland a handful of times. I absolutely love Ireland. I am not sure why really, but I do. This is a fun little poem that I wrote to Ireland.

To Ireland

Your rolling hills of emerald green
Blanketed with bursts of heather within.

The cliffs that stretch from ocean below
To tickle the cloud laden sky above.
Where wave and sea do crash.

Soft lilting tunes piped and strung
Entrance my soul to thee
With thee my heart doth find
A true affinity.

The Story behind "Try, Try, Try"...

We all have bad days, but it is those bad days that the Lord is with us. If we can try our best to give what we can then He makes up the rest. We give ten percent and He makes up the other ninety.

One of my favorite quotes;

"In the Gospel of Jesus Christ we get credit for trying, but we really have to try."

-President Gordon B. Hinckley

Try, Try, Try

Some days I don't want to get out of bed
I find it hard to place down my weary feet
But, within the steady pace of my heart's beat
A quiet voice, softly speaks.

Just try your best and I will be there
Lifting you up when you cannot dare-
To lift another finger
To even stare
I am here as you reach the end of your line
All I ask is
Try, try, try.

The Story behind "Walking By Faith"...

I wrote this poem as I was newly back in the church. People sometimes say that Christians have blind faith, but I believe that we see the most clear as we put our faith in the One who can see the best, even our Lord, Jesus Christ.

"For we walk by faith, and not by sight."

Walking By Faith

With faith in Him
I reach out my hand
Immediately it is enveloped
Fitting snug inside of His.
He knowingly leads me down the path
That leads to joy for me.

My eyes are shrouded
With love for Him
I cannot see a thing
But this I know
Without a shadow
No harm shall befall me.

His light illuminates my life
Giving me courage to
Fearlessly choose faith
With confidence firmly declare,
"Yes, I will follow thee, dear Lord."

For I know that Thou
Wouldst never lead me astray
I know that with each and every
Footstep taken in faith
I am blessed day by day.

The Story behind "Warrior"...

When I knew that I was supposed to write a book of poems this was the first one I wrote. The Plan of Happiness is simple. It was presented to us by a loving Father in heaven before this life. Agency-the power to choose between right and wrong-is the most important thing. Freedom to choose: righteousness and life, or wickedness and death. Satan wanted to take away that free choice.

The plan is this: We come to Earth to get a body and gain life experience. While we are on this Earth we learn to follow our Lord and Savior Jesus Christ. We follow His example by getting baptized by somebody who holds the proper Priesthood authority- or the power from God. After we are baptized we receive the gift of the Holy Ghost- a Member of the Godhead who can be with us as a constant friend, teacher, guide, and lifeguard of sorts. We keep the commandments of God and love those around us. We accept Jesus as our Savior and He then can save us. When we die we go to either Spirit Prison or Spirit Paradise. Prison is more like a waiting room where you have another opportunity to choose to follow Jesus Christ if you didn't get the proper chance on Earth. Those who go to Spirit Paradise are those who were baptized while in mortality and followed their Savior and walked uprightly before God. They help those in spirit Prison learn these things. We are then judged by the One who knows our hearts, and assigned a Kingdom of glory: Celestial, Terrestrial, or Telestial

Warrior

I can almost remember a time
Not too long ago,
When hearts were untroubled
When we were not even souls.
A spirit is all that was me;
A spirit who loved to be free.

There was more. We could tell.
We wanted to be like Father and Mother-
Full of Divine glory.
So...

The Father who loved us so much in His heart
Shared a new plan
To help us. Fully, and not just in part,
To become more like Him
To live and to grow.

We shouted for Joy!
You and me
That day that He shared the plan
The plan to be happy.

How lovely, how grand!
The plan would ensue
Helping us become
More
More like the Father we loved.

One was all it took
To shake, shake, shake
Our World and the New born plan
Like a fish off a hook, the ripples they shook

He rebelled out of pride and
Fear was there too.
He just couldn't see
From his limited view
The whole picture,
With its grand beauty.

Many would follow
Schemes. Lies.
Many would falter
Just to realize
The Father was willing to give
All He had
But still,
They wanted what they wanted
To have.

Father called those
Who were willing to find
Our brothers, our sisters
Those who so poorly chose
To follow the False One
The traitor to us all.

So, behind enemy lines
We willingly went.
Warriors in our might
Valiant Spirits.

We fought not
For glory nor pride but,
A treasure more precious
Than rubies and gold-
The hearts of our friends
Even their souls.

A war commenced
It was us against them.
No weapon was grander
Than the one that we bolstered,
Our testimony of
Father, and His great Plan
Jesus Christ as our
Chosen Savior.

Our testimonies shone
With the majesty and luster
Of the bright, bright starlight,
Dispelling the darkness that
Invaded Heaven that night.

With weapon in hand
We fought through the night
When dawn finally broke
The truth was bespoke

We had won the fight
The Good and the Light,
Still with a great cost to be borne.
A loss of the third.
Deception won within their lives.

We mourned their loss,
The ones that we loved.
Our brothers
Our sisters
Our dear dear friends.
Cast away and cast out
From us and from Heaven.
Cast out, cast out
Cast out for rebellion.

The Plan went forward
We continued to follow
Our Brother,
Our Lord,
Our chosen Savior.
To Earth We were born
Running through the veil,
Hounding our lives
As they were just beginning.

The terrain might have changed
Still the same battle raged.
The War in Heaven
Followed us to Earth
As the moon pulls the tide
Along the sea line.

Every day we fight
For the treasure to keep.
Not rubies,
Not diamonds,
Not even some gold,
Much more important.
The prize of our souls.

Warriors on Earth
Warriors in Heaven
Fighting right beside
Right beside the other.

Fighting for freedom from
Entangling nets
Of sin and of Hell,
That would trap us like light
In a sinking black hole.

Warriors we were
We still are today.
We pick up our swords
With our shields
Every. Single. Day.

We fight with our might and
The knowledge we have:
Our Savior fights beside us
Every breath that we live.

The Story behind "What if I Lost My Chance"...

When we love somebody we have to let them know. We need to show that love by word and deed every day. We never know when it will be our turn to leave this life, so we must make the most of it. Make the most out of those moments with the ones we love. We might not get another chance.

What if I Lost My Chance?

What if something happened
That took you away from me?
What if I never got to
See you one more day?

Would I recognize then
My one lost chance?
Would I understand
That I
Just let my opportunity
Pass right on by?

If I never could see
Your smiling eyes
Or hear your warm laugh
I would indeed
Regret my lost chance.

I would realize then
Just a little
Too late,
That I should have borne
My heart to you
And loved you
A little more each day.

The Story behind "When the Days Are Long"...

This one was written on my mission as well. I was emailing my Mom and this just came out. It was my raw feelings at the time.

When the Days Are Long

Have I ever told you how much I really love you?
Or when I am not having a not so good day, I think
of you and pray?
Or when I am tired and have given all I have, I think
of you and how you are blessed when I press on,
persevere in my best.

I struggle in this work.
Some days more than some, but as I think of who I
am I know I can press on.
Not only am I your daughter, friend, granddaughter,
and niece;
I am a daughter of a king.

He called me to this noble, mighty, and great
responsibility.
To stand as a witness in all places
Firm and strong, my only duty to give my best and
keep pressing on.
I represent my Savior, in all I do and say and try my
hardest to be like Him
As He would be today.

I cannot slack or lessen my pace or take a break to
breathe.
For it is my mandate to serve my Lord and witness
His great name.
To save the precious souls of all my brothers and
sisters.
At that great day bring them unto him.

For all the bruises and scratches on my heart, I
cannot give up now.
I have to do my part.
For there are now, in many darkened places, those
who know not who they are, or that they are not
forsaken
That they too have a part.
A part to play in this grand place, this world, our
trying grounds.
This place called Earth, a school for us to grow and
learn.
That these my friends are just waiting to be found.
•

This is the work that I have been called to do, and is
my earnest desire.
To impart to my dear friends this living water.
But when I get tired or think I cannot go on, I think
of all the blessings that for them can be won.
Also, from my earnest efforts the blessings you
receive and the protection that is over you as I daily
succeed.

So, I do not dare let up, or think I cannot do.
For I know the reason I serve is because I love him
and I love you!
All of you have a place within my ever-growing
heart.
To me you are the reason for my life and the very
most precious part.
I love you more than you can even think and more
than you even know.
So, when life is hard, as it is wont to be, remember
that I love you and truly believe.

I believe that you can carry all the burdens you are
called to shoulder.
Believe, though you might not think so, our Savior is
there carrying part.
Part of you burdens and the load that you are called
to bear.
He is always with you and always standing there.

He is always standing right beside you, helping you
along
Standing right beside you when the days are long.
Know that I love you, but more importantly, that He
who truly died for you, loves you too.
Take care my precious part, and know that you are
always in my heart.

The Story behind "Within a Tear"...

I have often said that a person is most beautiful when they are crying, and it is true! The ability to cry is a gift. Crying releases emotions that would otherwise get stuck inside of us and cause problems. In the scriptures it says,

"Jesus wept" – John 11:35

If Jesus wept than I am sure we can too. It is important.

Within a Tear

Within a tear
There is sometimes fear
And pain
And sorrow
But other times...
Other times there are
Moments of hope
Hope for tomorrow.

A single tear contains
Much much more
Than just salt and water.
That teardrop is a gift
It holds a certain power.

The spirit of our Lord
Dwells there
Within that drop, that gift
The ability to feel closer to God
Is held there,
Suspended gracefully there⁻
Within a tear.

Made in the USA
San Bernardino, CA
23 December 2018